Silly Riddles

Wacky Animal Riddles

by A. J. Sautter

PEBBLE
a capstone imprint

Published by Pebble, an imprint of Capstone
1710 Roe Crest Drive
North Mankato, Minnesota 56003
capstonepub.com

Copyright © 2024 by Capstone. All rights reserved. No part of this publication may be reproduced in whole or in part, or stored in a retrieval system, or transmitted in any form or by any means, electronic, mechanical, photocopying, recording, or otherwise, without written permission of the publisher.

Library of Congress Cataloging-in-Publication Data is available on the Library of Congress web site.
ISBN 9780756574789 (library binding)
ISBN 9780756574734 (paperback)
ISBN 9780756574741 (ebook PDF)

Summary: A collection of silly riddles about animals for young readers.

Editorial Credits
Editor: Aaron Sautter; Designer: Jaime Willems; Media Researcher: Rebekah Hubstenberger; Production Specialist: Whitney Schaefer

Photo Credits
Shutterstock: asawinimages, 12, BearFotos, 21, colnihko, design element (color eye), Eric Isselee, 7, 11, 15, 19, 20, fivespots, 13, geraldb, 4, GoodFocused, 8, Happy monkey, 5, IrinaK, cover (bottom left), Liliya Butenko, 16, NATALIA61, design element (googly eye), Nynke van Holten, 18, oksanka007, design element (paper cutouts), Perfectorius, design element (symbols), Pixfiction, 10, Sergii Figurnyi, 14, sevenke, cover (bottom right), 1, Smit, cover (top right), StockArtRoom, design element (shapes), Tim UR, 9, Valdis Skudre, 6, Yes058 Montree Nanta, 17

All internet sites appearing in back matter were available and accurate when this book was sent to press.

Printed in the United States   5801

Table of Contents

Furry Funnies 4
Wild Stumpers 10
Beastly Mind-Benders 16
Glossary 22
Read More 23
Internet Sites 23
Index 24
About the Author 24

Words in **bold** are in the glossary.

Furry Funnies

1. I hide my **treasure** underground like a pirate. But I have a bushy tail. What am I?

2. Is it hard to spot a leopard?

Answers!

1. A squirrel.
2. Not really—they already come with spots!

3. How do rabbits stay so cute and fluffy?

4. Why couldn't the cat use his new computer?

Answers!

3. They use hare spray.

4. Because he ate the mouse.

5. Why does a giraffe always arrive late to parties?

6. Why are ponies and horses such terrible dancers?

Answers!

5. He has to wash his neck first.
6. Because they have two left feet.

7. What tool would a gorilla use to fix a leaky pipe?

8. What do you call a little bear who never takes a bath?

Answers!

7. A monkey wrench.

8. Winnie the pee-yew.

9. What happened when the kangaroo found his sister sneaking around in his room?

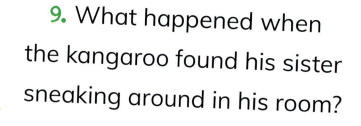

10. What are two things that a lion can never eat for breakfast?

Answers!

9. He got hopping mad.
10. Lunch and dinner.

8

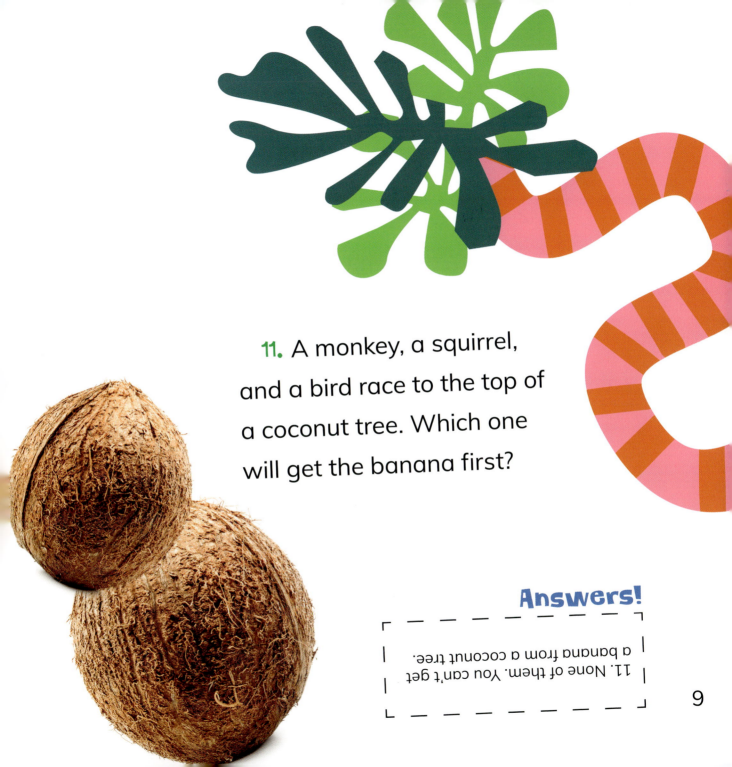

11. A monkey, a squirrel, and a bird race to the top of a coconut tree. Which one will get the banana first?

Answers!

11. None of them. You can't get a banana from a coconut tree.

Wild Stumpers

12. What animal should you call if you want to do an old-time square dance at the beach?

Answers!

12. A fiddler crab.

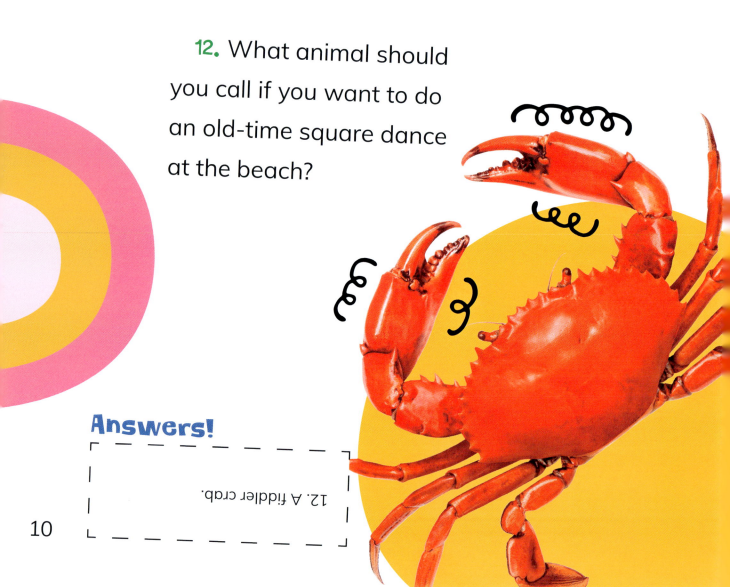

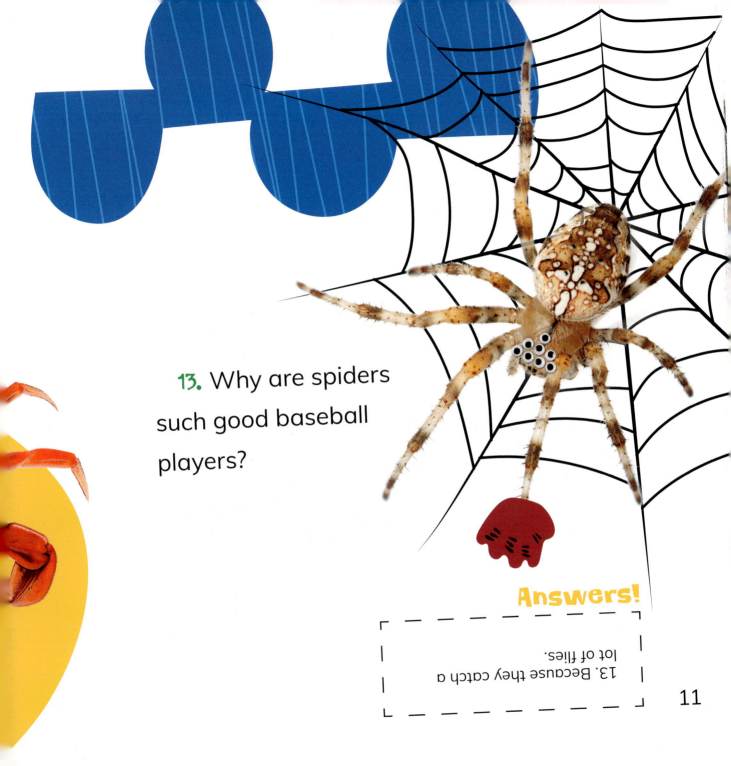

13. Why are spiders such good baseball players?

Answers!

13. Because they catch a lot of flies.

11

14. Where should a frog go if he's feeling sick?

15. What happened to the frog's car after it broke down on the road?

Answers!

14. To the hospital.
15. It got toad away!

16. What's the best way to make a **poisonous** snake cry?

Answers!

16. Take away its rattle.

17. How are an elephant and a tall tree alike?

18. What happened to the cat that ate a whole ball of yarn?

Answers!

17. They both have long trunks.
18. She had a litter of mittens.

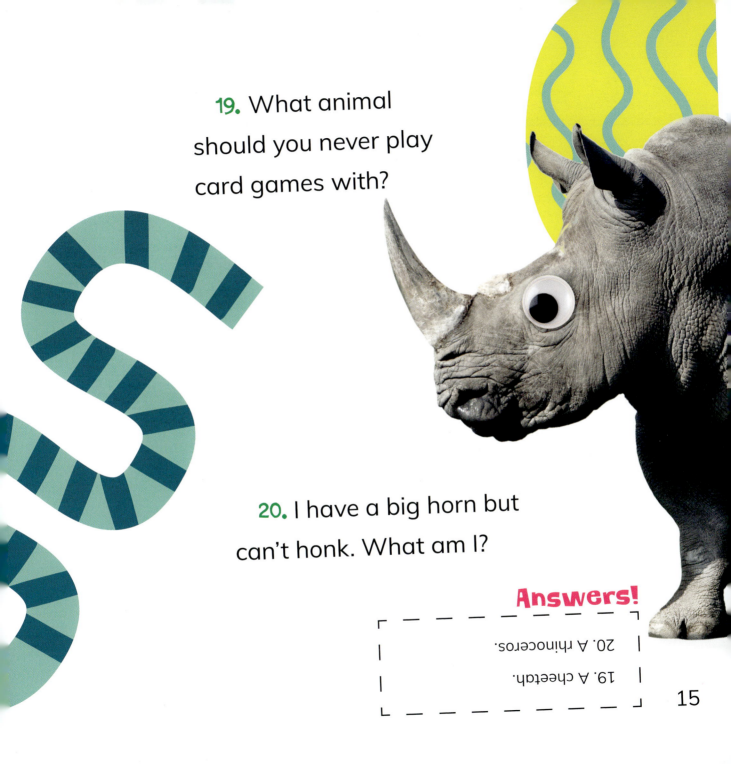

19. What animal should you never play card games with?

20. I have a big horn but can't honk. What am I?

Answers!

19. A cheetah.
20. A rhinoceros.

15

Beastly Mind-Benders

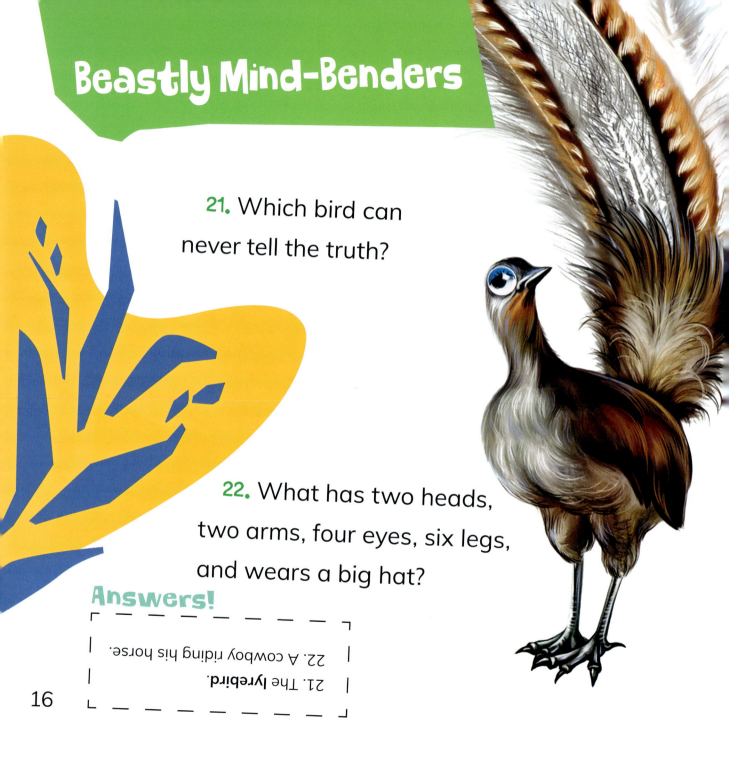

21. Which bird can never tell the truth?

22. What has two heads, two arms, four eyes, six legs, and wears a big hat?

Answers!

21. The **lyrebird**.
22. A cowboy riding his horse.

16

23. Tony the giant **tortoise** is 6 years old. His sister, Tonya Tortoise, is half his age. When Tony is 40 years old, how old will Tonya Tortoise be?

Answers!

23. 37 years old.

17

24. Multiply this number of cats by any other number and you always get the same answer. What number of cats is this?

25. What is black and white, black and white, black and white, and green?

Answers!

24. Zero cats.

25. Three skunks eating a pickle.

26. A donkey is tied to a 6-foot (1.8-meter) rope. A **bale** of hay is 20 feet (6 m) away. How can the donkey eat the hay?

Answers!

26. Easily. The other end of the rope is not tied to anything.

27. I jump when I walk and sit when I stand. What am I?

28. What grows **down** while it's growing up?

Answers!

27. A kangaroo.
28. A goose.

29. Two eyes in front, but many eyes behind. What animal am I?

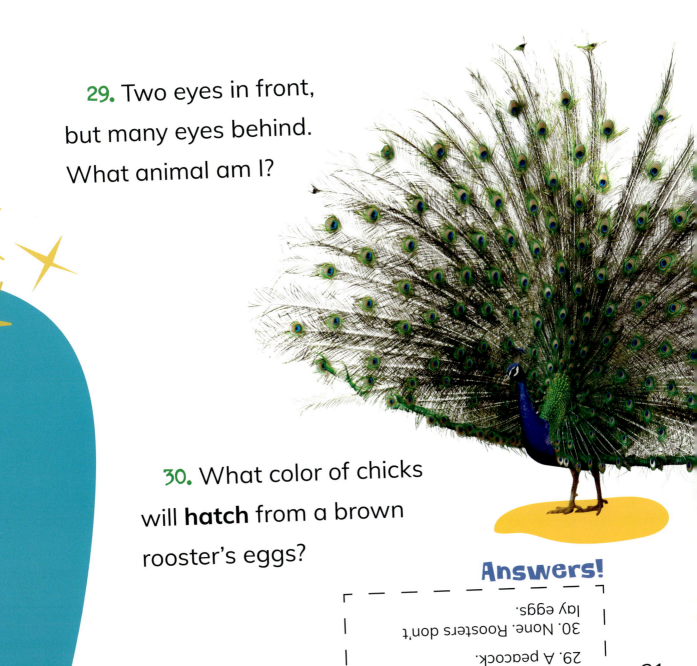

30. What color of chicks will **hatch** from a brown rooster's eggs?

Answers!

29. A peacock.
30. None. Roosters don't lay eggs.

Glossary

bale (BAYL)—a large bundle of straw or hay tied tightly together

down (DOWN)—the soft, fluffy feathers on a bird

hatch (HACH)—to break out of an egg

lyrebird (LAHY-uhr-burd)—a bird that lives in Australia; male lyrebirds have long, colorful tails

poisonous (POI-zuhn-uhss)—able to harm or kill with poison or venom

tortoise (TOR-tuhss)—a turtle that lives only on land

treasure (TREZH-uhr)—gold, jewels, or other valuable items that are often hidden

Read More

Highlights. *501 Backyard Animal Joke-Tivities: Riddles, Puzzles, Fun Facts, Cartoons, Tongue Twisters, and Other Giggles!* Honesdale, PA: Highlights Press, 2022.

Dahl, Michael. *Silly Jokes About Animals.* North Mankato, MN: Pebble, 2022.

Huddleston, Emma. *Animal Riddles.* Mankato, MN: The Child's World, 2022.

Internet Sites

45 Animal Riddles That are Bear-Y Puzzling
kidadl.com/funnies/riddles/animal-riddles-that-are-bear-y-puzzling

55 Animal Riddles for Kids and Adults
ponly.com/animal-riddles/

100 Funny Animal Riddles
icebreakerideas.com/animal-riddles/

Index

bears, 7
birds, 9, 16, 20, 21

cats, 5, 14, 18
cheetahs, 15
crabs, 10

donkeys, 19

elephants, 14

frogs, 12

giraffes, 6
gorillas, 7

horses, 6, 16

kangaroos, 8, 20

leopards, 4
lions, 8

monkeys, 9

rabbits, 5
rhinoceroses, 15

skunks, 18
snakes, 13
spiders, 11
squirrels, 4, 9

tortoises, 17

About the Author

A. J. Sautter is an author and editor of dozens of kid's books on everything from aliens to zombies. He lives in Minnesota with his wife and children. He enjoys reading, going to the movies, and going for long walks with his fluffy, adorable dogs.